AUSSIE SLANG

WORDS & PHRASES

The "Aussie Slang Words" guidebook takes you through the journey of the Australian language. Packed with over 300 words and phrases, this mini guide comes complete with definitions and examples for use in real life situations. Engage with the illustrations to embrace and expand your vocabulary of Aussie slang.

Spot On

Perfect, exactly.

"That barbie was spot on."

After Dark

Rhyming slang for shark.

"I saw an after dark at the beach."

Brickie

Bricklayer.

"I got a job as a brikkie."

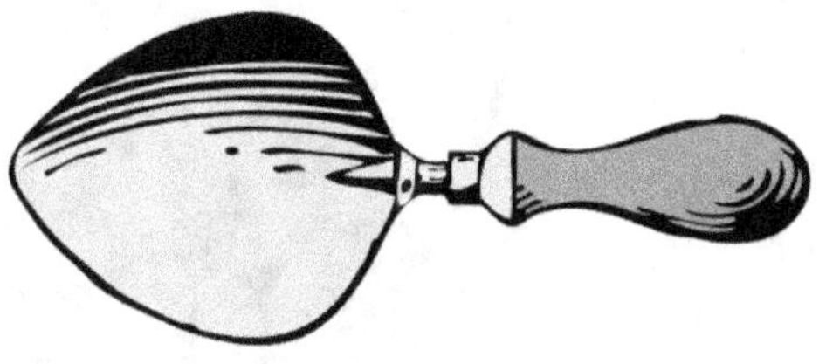

All Piss And Wind

Full of shit.

"You're all piss and wind mate."

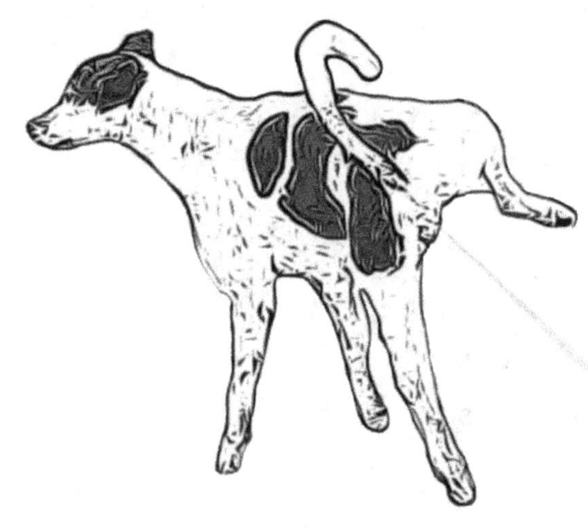

Perve

Looking lustfully at the opposite sex.

"That sheila is perving at you."

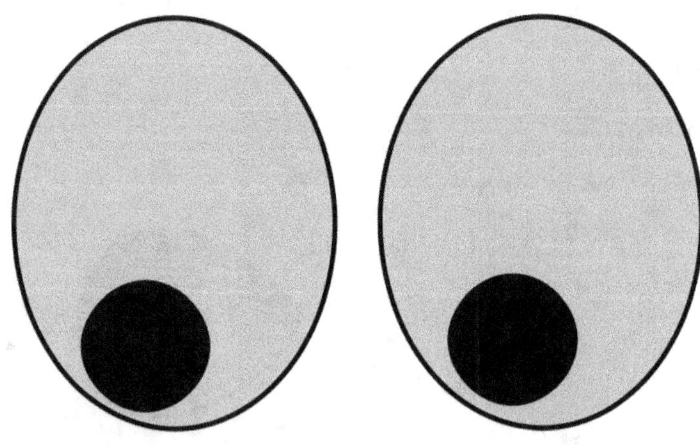

Buckley's Chance

No chance.

"You have Buckley's chance of finding a ticket."

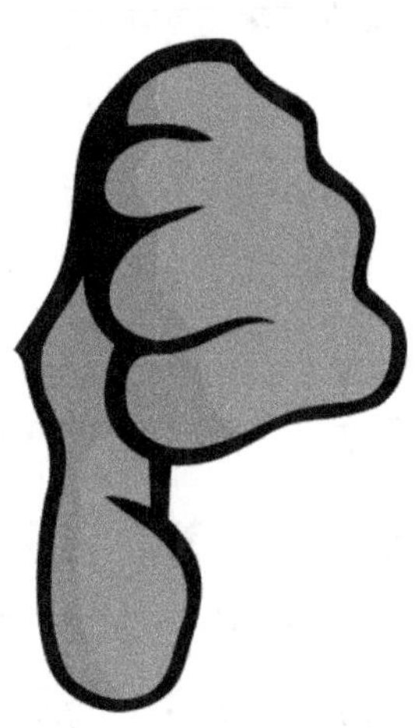

Give It A Burl

Try it, have a go.

"Give it a burl, you might like it."

Fly Wire

Gauze flyscreen covering a window or doorway.

"Definitely need a fly wire by the front door."

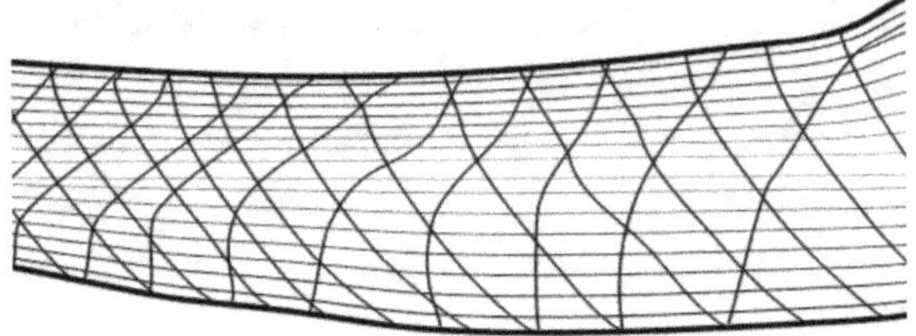

Dust Eaters

People who live in the Northern Territory.

"Dust eaters love going to the South."

Knock

To criticise.

"Don't knock it until you try it."

Roo

Kangaroo.

"The new restaurant does a fantastic roo burger."

Hooroo

Goodbye.

"Hooroo, see you tomorrow."

Cook

Someone's wife.

"I'll have to ask the cook if I can go out tonight."

Clayton's

Fake.

"Those shoes are Clayton's."

Get The Pink Slip

Get the sack. It is the colour of the termination form.

"He got the pink slip for being late all week."

Prezzy

Present, gift.

"I still need to buy her Chrissie prezzy yet."

Brown-Eyed Mullet

A turd in the sea (also bondi cigar).

"I don't who left a brown-eyed mullet there again."

Aerial Pingpong

Australian Rules Football.

"Let's play some aerial pingpong."

___

Drink With The Flies

To drink alone.

"I was drinking with the flies because she didn't turn up."

___

Kip

A short nap.

"I'm off for a kip for an hour."

___

<u>Boomer</u>

A large kangaroo.

"I've never seen a boomer that big before."

<u>Gander</u>

To have a look at.

"Let's have a gander at your new phone."

Yabby

Inland freshwater crayfish found in Australia.

"I want to catch some yabbies for dinner."

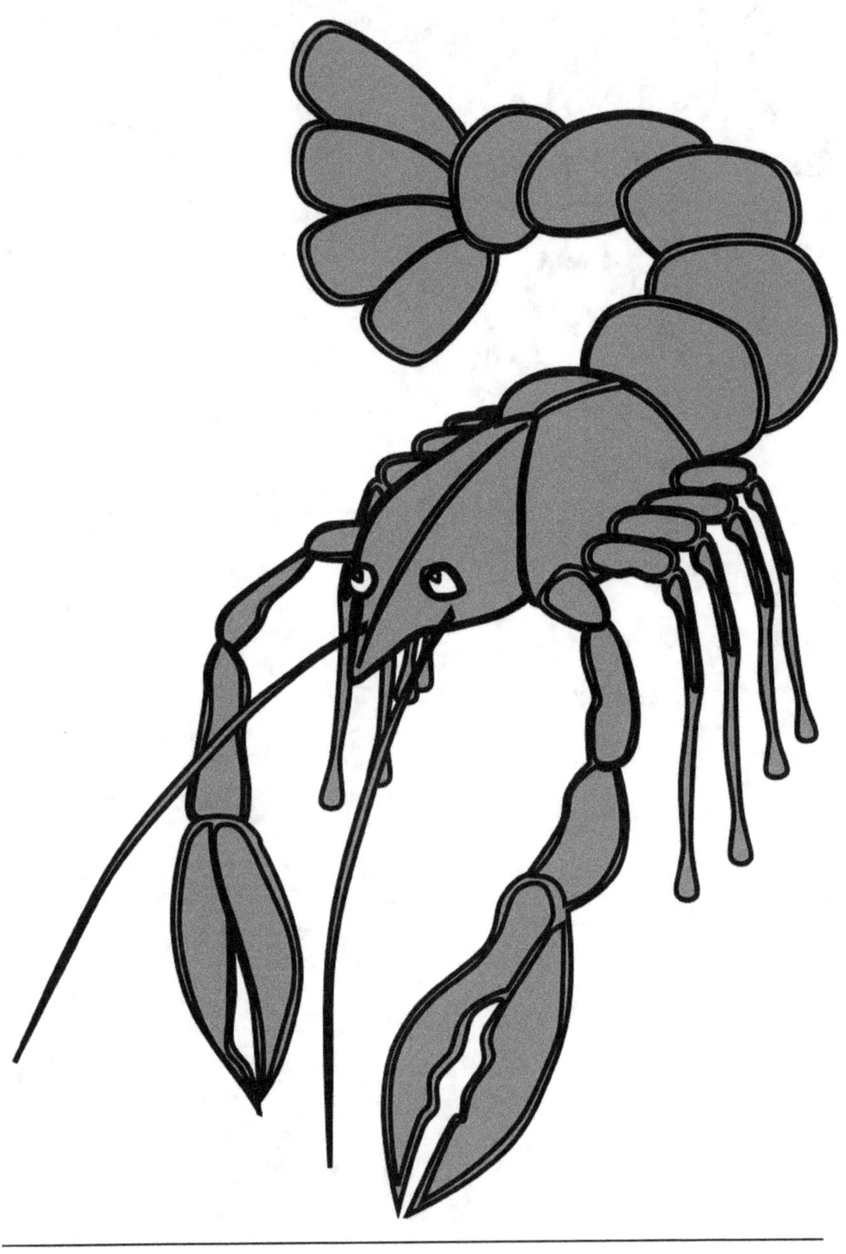

Technicolor Yawn

Vomit.

"The technicolor yawn was worth the bonza night."

Offsider

An assistant, helper.

"My offsider has chucked a sickie again."

As Dry As A Dead Dingo's Donger

Very dry.

"This sausage is as dry as a dead dingo's donger."

Cattle Duffer

A cattle thief.

"There was a cattle duffer on the loose."

Digger

An Australian soldier.

"He managed to pass his fitness test and is now a digger."

Mad As A Cut Snake

Very angry.

"She was as mad as a cut snake when she saw he drew all over the freshly painted walls."

Crikey

An expression of surprise.

"Crikey it's a cold 25 degrees today."

Ripper

An exclamation to describe something great or fantastic.

"What a ripper that dance move was."

Bingle

Motor vehicle accident.

"I was involved in a bingle yesterday."

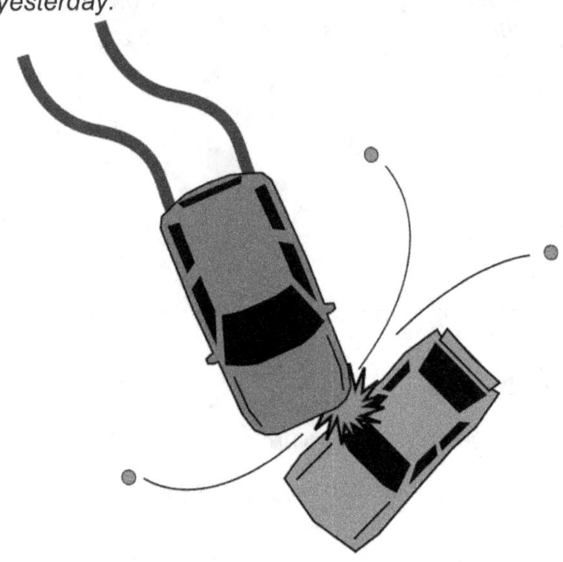

As Dry As A Pommy's Towel

Very dry (based on a pom bathing once a month).

"My mouth is as dry as a Pommy's towel."

Outback

The very remote interior areas of Australia.

"We're heading through the outback for an adventure."

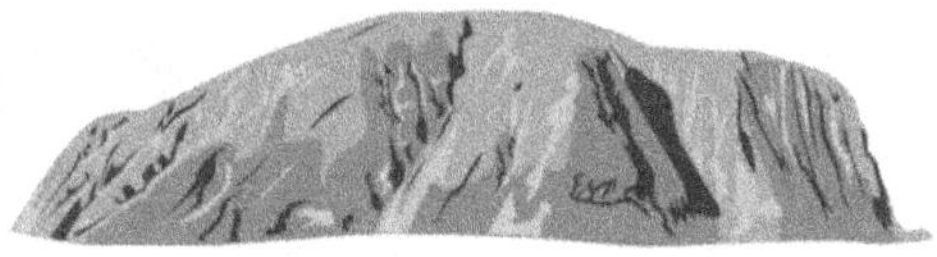

Dob In

Inform on somebody.

"I'll dob you in if you don't listen."

Nasho

National service.

"He won't be good at nasho."

Do The Harold Holt

To bolt.

"Do the Harold before we get soaked by the rain."

Clod Hoppers

Feet.

"My clod hoppers ache after the walk."

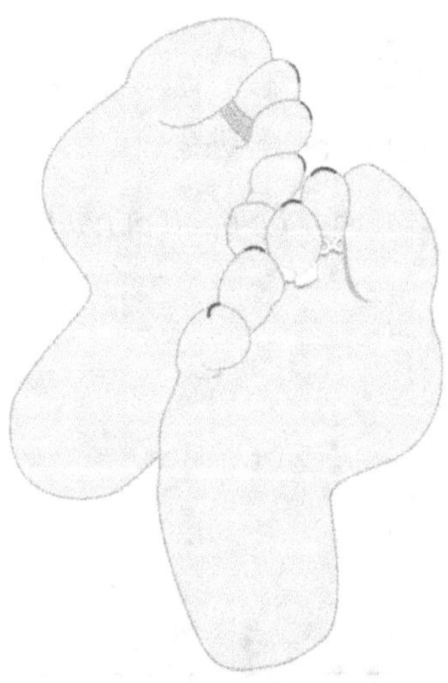

Surfies

People who go surfing.

"Surfies are out until sunset."

Bouncy Mouse

Kangaroo.

"There was a bouncy mouse in the garden."

Dog

An unattractive woman.

"I wouldn't say she's a dog."

Bread Basket

Your stomach.

"You've got a large bread basket."

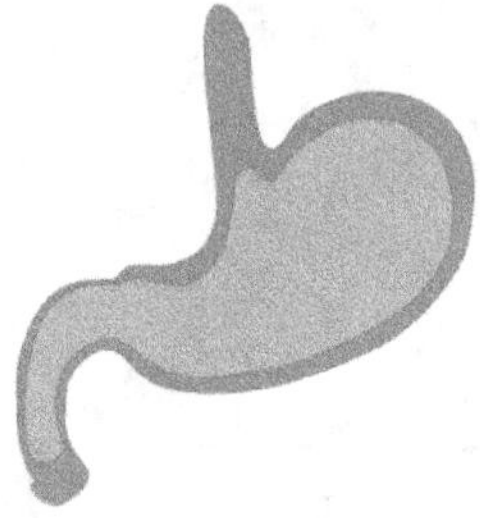

Choom

Englishman.

"The choom is sunburnt."

London To A Brick

Absolute certainty.

"He's going to pull tonight, London to a brick."

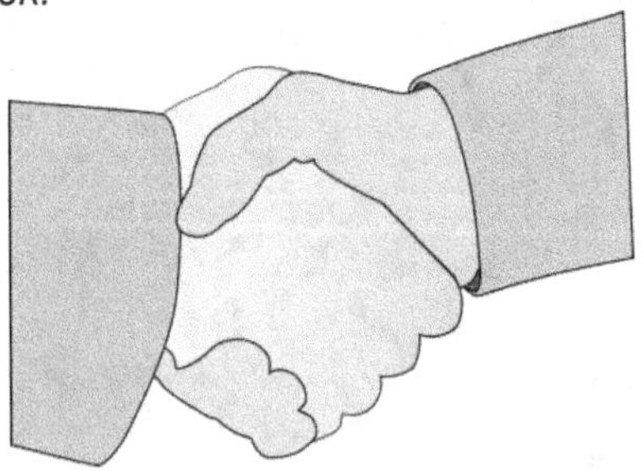

Brisvegas

Brisbane, Queensland.

"There aren't as many lights in Brisvegas."

Dingbat

A fool or immature person.

"Stop it you dingbat."

Root Rat

Somebody who is constantly looking for sex.

"The root rat is always going after different girls."

Local Rag

The local newspaper.

"The local rag never has any good stories."

Vinnie's

St. Vincent De Paul's (charity thrift stores and hostels).

"I found a bargain at Vinnie's yesterday."

Strewth

Exclamation, mild oath.

"Strewth, did you see the size of that roo?"

Australia's Little Brother

New Zealand.

"We're visiting Australia's little brother next month."

As Mean As Cat's Piss

Mean, stingy or uncharitable.

"You're as mean as cat's piss sometimes."

Clacker

Anus.

"Get your clacker moving."

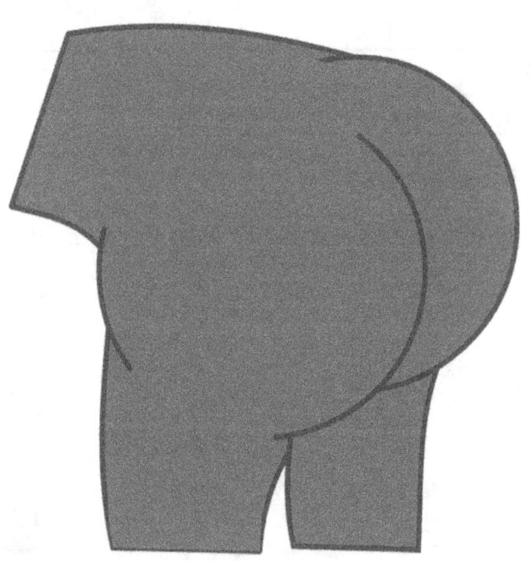

Bushweek

An exclamation that you don't believe what they are telling you.

"That is a load of bushweek."

Dead Horse

Rhyming slang for tomato sauce.

"Pass the dead horse."

Cackleberry

An egg.

"I want a cackleberry."

As Fit As A Mallee Bull

Very fit and strong.

"Look at him, as fit as a Mallee bull."

Cabbage Patcher

Resident of Victoria.

"He's a cabbage patcher."

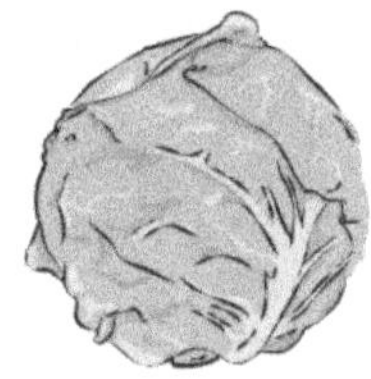

Swag

Rolled up bedding etc. by hikers or travelers.

"Pack your swag for the hike."

Jug

Electric kettle.

"Fill the jug."

<u>Flake</u>

Shark's flesh sold in fish & chips shops.

"We had flake on chips at the beach."

<u>Sprung</u>

Caught doing something wrong.

"He got sprung when he tried to sneak in after dark."

<u>Jackaroo</u>

A male trainee station manager or station hand.

"He's gone to be a jackaroo at the big station."

No Hoper

Somebody who'll never do well.

"He's a real no hoper spending all day sleeping."

Tall Poppies

Successful people.

"She was always the tall poppy in school."

Stubby Holder

Polystyrene insulated holder for a stubby.

"Make sure you bring the stubby holder, it's hot out there."

Good Nick

In good condition.

"The car is in good nick."

All Wool And A Yard Wide

Authentic and trustworthy.

"I always knew you were all wool and a yard wide."

Cut Lunch

Sandwiches.

"I can't think of anything else so a cut lunch will have to do."

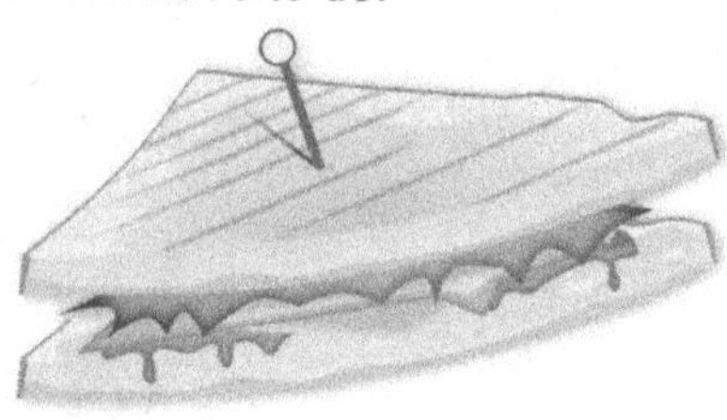

Plodder

Slow and steady worker.

"He's a plodder but he gets the job done."

Larrikin

A bloke who is always enjoying himself, a harmless prankster.

"He is a larriking, always making us laugh."

Bust A Gut

Work hard or to put in effort.

"I really bust a gut today."

Mickey Mouse

Somethingn that is not very good.

"His cooking was Mickey Mouse."

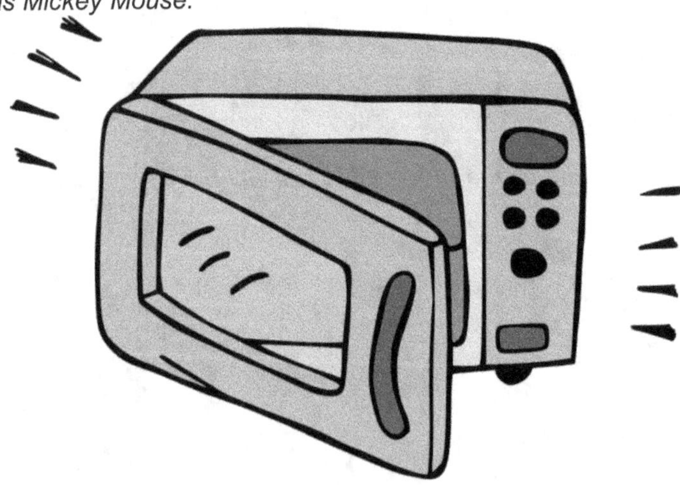

Dingo's Breakfast

No breakfast.

"I was late this morning and had a dongo's breakfast."

It Cost Big Bikkies

It was expensive.

"The plane ticket cost big bikkies."

Fang It

Drive fast.

"Fang it before the light turns red."

Funny As A Fart In An Elevator

Not funny.

"He's as funny as a fart in an elevator."

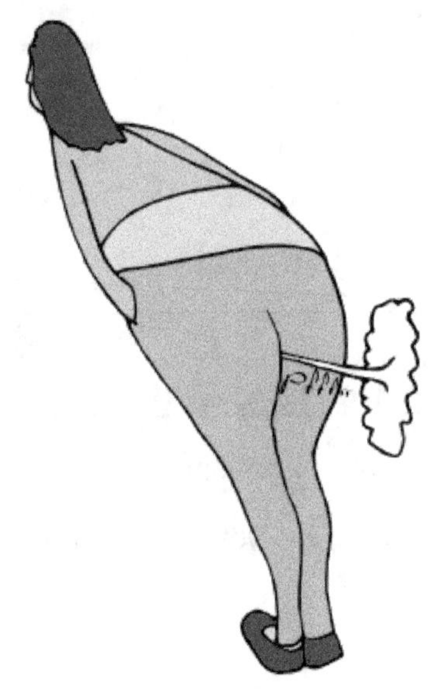

Lamington

Sponge cake cut into squares and covered in chocolate and coconut.

"We had a Lamington with a cuppa."

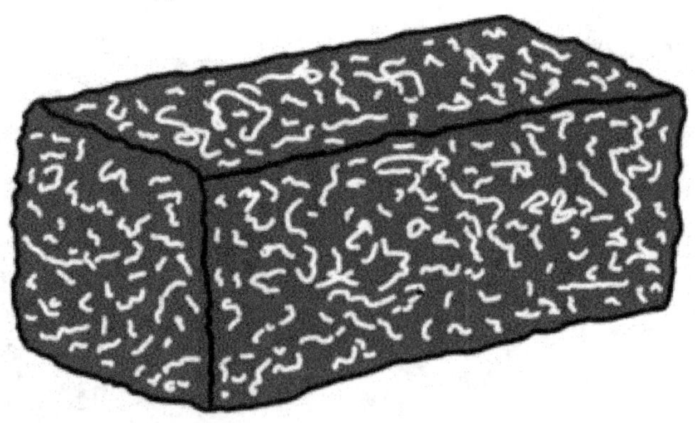

You Little Ripper

Exclamation of delight or as a reaction to good news.

"I won the competition. You little ripper!"

Fairy Floss

Candy floss.

"Fairy floss is also known as cotton candy in the US."

Garlic Muncher

Someone from Central or Southern Europe.

"The garlic muncher was talking in Spanish."

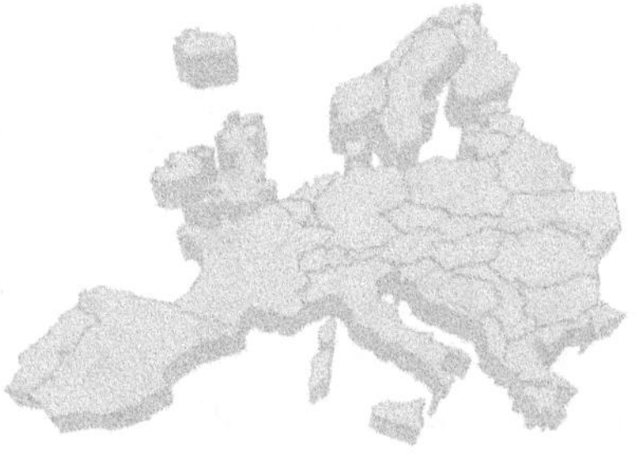

Nong

Idiot.

"You can be a right nong sometimes."

Ipshit

Ipswich, Queensland.

"Ipshit looks as good as it sounds."

Chook

A chicken.

"I've put a chook in the oven for dinner."

Nut Out

Work out something.

"We finally nutted out how to get there using a map."

Bizzo

Business.

"Mind your own bizzo."

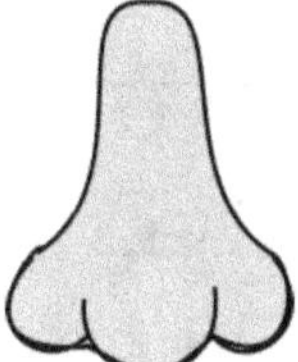

Booze Bus

Police vehicle used for catching drunk drivers.

"There's a booze bus around the corner."

Ratbag

Mild insult.

"The ratbag was caught stealing."

Clucky

Feeling broody or maternal.

"She's getting clucky for another one."

Bastard

A term of endearment.

"Hello you little bastard."

Bathers

Swimming costume.

"Get your bathers on and let's get in the pool."

Oldies

Parents.

"The oldies are away for the weekend."

Gregory Peck

Neck.

"My Gregory Peck is in pain."

Rellie

Family relative.

"The rellies are coming to stay."

<u>**Flick It On**</u>

To sell something, usually for a quick profit, soon after buying it.

"I bought it for 5 bucks and flicked it on for 20."

<u>**Ropeable**</u>

Very angry.

"She was ropeable when I told her about breaking the dishwasher."

<u>**Cark It**</u>

To die or stop functioning.

"The over has carked it."

Rort

Cheating, fiddling, defrauding. It is usually used of politicians.

"He tried to rort the system by trying to claim a refund."

Dinkum, Fair Dinkum

True, real, genuine.

"That's a fair dinkum meat pie."

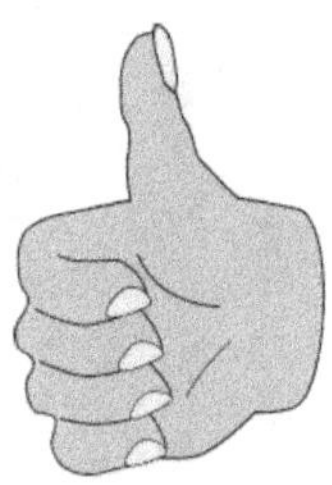

Not Within Cooee

A long way away or far off.

"You're not within cooee with that wild guess."

Rotten

Drunk.

"She was rotten by 9pm."

Docket

A bill or receipt.

"The docket shows how much we got charged."

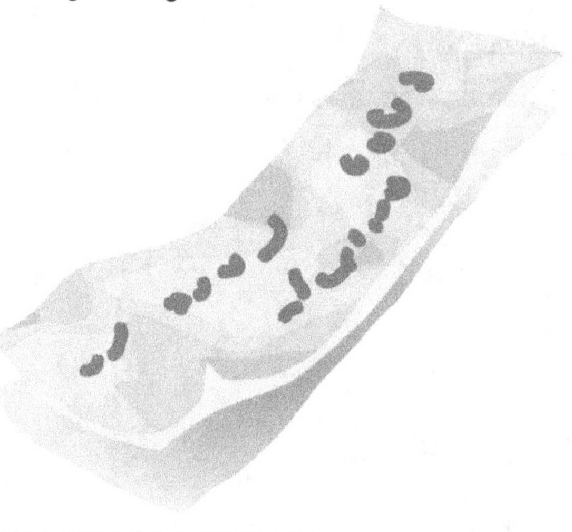

Not The Full Quid

Of low IQ.

"He put the bottle of water in the oven. He's obviously not the full quid."

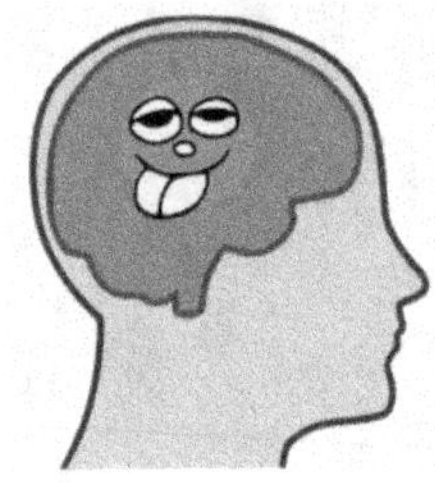

Vejjo

Vegetarian.

"She's decided to go full vejjo now."

Gasbag

A person who talks a lot.

"She is a gasbag when she gets together with her mates."

Op Shop

Opportunity shop. a place where second hand goods are sold.

"I bought this handbag from the op shop and it was only 5 bucks!"

Squizz

To look at something.

"I'm going to squizz at the bargains."

Down Under

Australia and New Zealand.

"We're from down under."

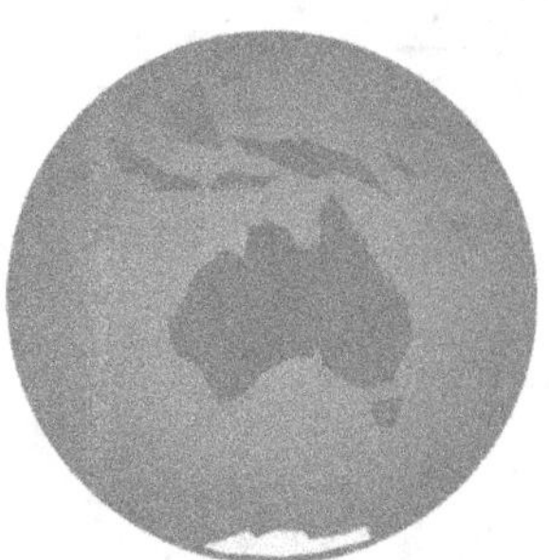

Sav

Saveloy.

"Throw another sav on the barbie mate."

Cranny

Cranbourne, Victoria.

"Cranny is a wonderful place."

Sickie

Day off sick from work.

"She decided to chuck a sickie after a night out drinking."

Avos

Avocados.

"The avos are nice and ripe."

Dropped Your Guts

You have farted.

"Is that you who has dropped your guts?"

Waggin' School

Playing truant.

"He was waggin' school and spent the day at the beach."

Ozzies

Australians.

"Ozzies are used to battling with mozzies."

Bitzer

Mongrel dog.

"She had a bitzer."

Bring A Plate

Instruction on a party or barbecue invitation to bring your own food.

"You're invited to the party tomorrow. Bring a plate."

He Hasn't Got A Brass Razoo

He's very poor.

"He didn't buy the tickets because he hasn't got a brass razoo."

Heaps

A lot.

"If you visit in the summer you'll be sweating heaps."

Aussie Salute

Brushing away flies with the hand.

"He's was giving the Aussie salute all evening."

Jillaroo

A female trainee station manager or station hand.

"He wants to speak to the new jillaroo because he thinks she's a hornbag."

The Singing Budgie

Kylie Minogue.

"The singing budgie has a new single out and I can't get it out of my head."

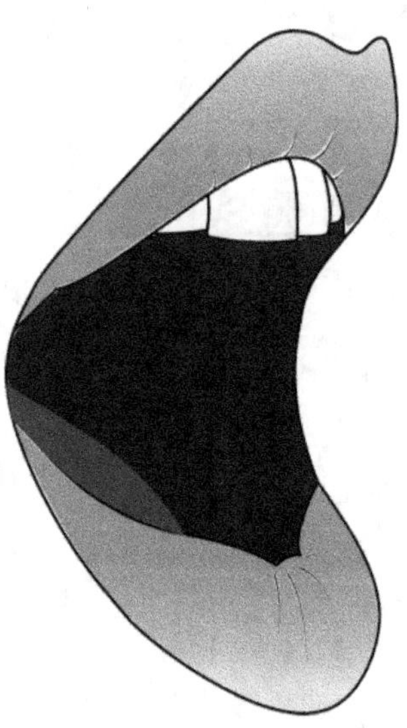

Crow Eater

A person from South Australia.

"He's a crow eater."

Mozzie

Mosquito.

"I got a mozzie bite when I was in the bush."

Chinwag

To have a lot of mostly friendly conversation with someone.

"We just had a huge chinwag."

The Lucky Country

Australia.

"I moved to the lucky country 5 years ago and have never looked back since."

Bodgy

Of inferior quality.

"Those tools are a bit bodgy."

Cockie

Cockroach.

"There is no cockie infestation here."

Buster

Strong wind.

"That buster nearly blew me off my feet."

Cobber

A good friend.

"How are you my old cobber?"

Brekkie

Breakfast.

"It's time for brekkie."

Egg On

Encourage or persuade a hesitant person.

"I was trying to egg him on but he wouldn't do it."

Sheila

A term for a woman.

"Ask that sheila over there."

Face Fungus

Beard.

"You need to get rid of your face fungus."

Tassie

Tasmania.

"Let's head to Tassie and sample the food there."

Tim Tam

A treat consisting of two chocolate malt biscuits joined together by a chocolate cream filling and coated in even more chocolate.

"You can't beat a Tim Tam with a cuppa."

Muster

A gathering of people or animals.

"We can have a muster next week to celebrate."

Sambo

Sandwich.

"I feel like a sambo for lunch today."

Bluey

Blue cattle dog (a working dog).

"Where's the bluey?"

Half Your Luck

Congratulations or best wishes.

"Half your luck tomorrow."

Brumby

A wild horse.

"A brumby is roaming the neighbourhood."

Furphy

False or unreliable rumour.

"Don't believe the furphy going round about me."

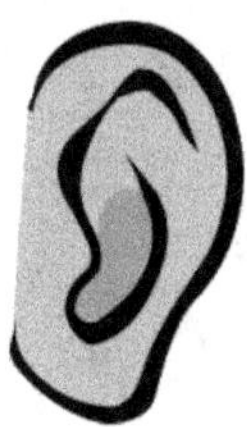

Cow Juice

Milk from a cow.

"We have run out of cow juice."

Septic Tank

Yank. Rhyming slang for an American. Seppo for short.

"The seppo was wearing a winter coat in this weather!"

Duds

Trousers.

"Where are my duds?"

Chips

French-fries.

"Sausage and chips is the best."

Hard Yakka

Hard work.

"It's always hard yakka when you're doing manual work."

Longneck

750ml bottle of beer in South Australia.

"A longneck beer is exactly what I need after a long day."

Dead-Cert

Definite or certain.

"Dead cert, it is going to be a scorcher tomorrow."

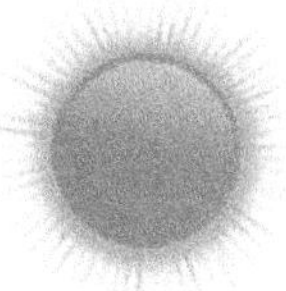

Oz

Australia.

"I can't wait to get back to Oz to see the sun again."

Alkie

An alcoholic.

"I wasn't an alkie until I turned 30."

Easterner

A Western Australian term for a person from the Eastern States.

"If you're an Easterner you're from the East."

Got The Wobbly Boot On

Drunk.

"One drink and she got the wobbly boot on."

Dole Bludger

Somebody on social assistance when unjustified.

"He hasn't had a job for years the dole bludger."

As Cross As A Frog In A Sock

A person sounding angry.

"He's as cross as a frog in a sock."

Yobbo

A person lacking good manners.

"He's a yobbo."

Freckle

Anus.

"That's a rather large freckle."

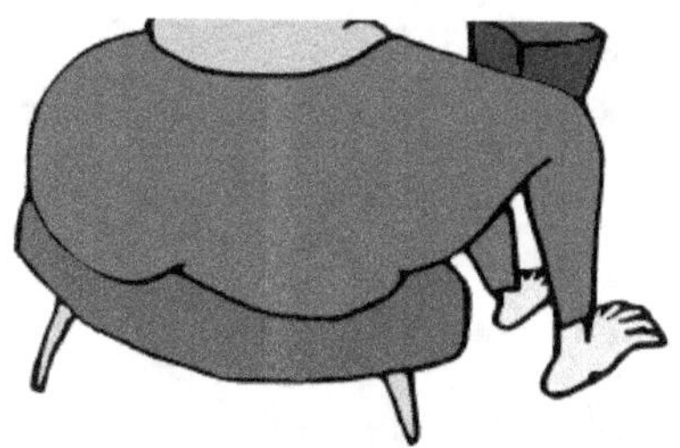

Blow In The Bag

Have a breathalyser test.

"I had to blow in the bag."

Hornbag

A very attractive person, typically a woman.

"I think she's a proper hornbag."

Cruisy

Easy.

"That was cuisy."

Bazzaland

Australia.

"Bazzaland is the best place in the world."

Bloody

Very.

"That's a bloody hairy face!"

Daks

Trousers.

"Your daks go over your underwear."

Back Of Bourke

A very long way away.

"The shop of back of Bourke."

Ambo

An ambulance or ambulance driver.

"Call an ambo quick!"

Chokkie

Chocolate.

"I eat way too much chokkie."

Stickybeak

Nosey person.

"The new neighbour is such a stickybeak mate."

Drongo

A term for a silly person.

"He's a bit of a drongo."

Tee-Up

To set up something like an appointment.

"I've got a tee-up for an arvo of sunbaking with the girls."

Bushwalking

Hiking or walking in the bush for pleasure.

"I love bushwalking."

Useful As An Ashtray On A Motorbike

Unhelpful or incompetent person or thing.

"Don't as her to bake you a cake. She's as useful as an ashtray on a motorbike."

Blowie

A blow fly.

"Look at that little blowie."

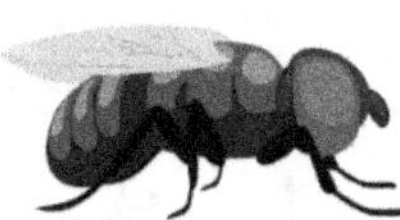

Truckie

Truck driver.

"The truckie pulled over for the night and sat back with a cold one."

Whinge

To complain.

"She's always whinging about the weather."

Tallie

750ml bottle of beer.

"A tallie, just what I needed in this arvo sun."

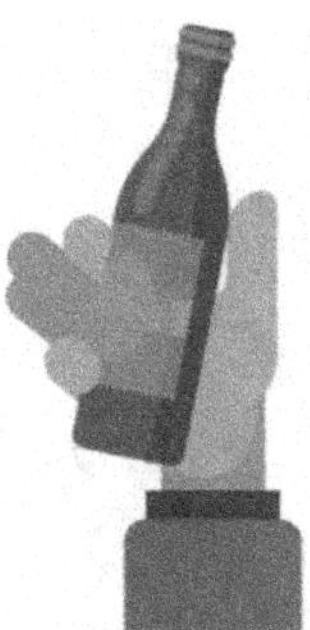

<u>Feral</u>

A wild person.

"He's just plain feral."

<u>Joey</u>

Baby kangaroo.

"The joey is too cute."

Didgeri-Don't

Stop.

"Didgeri-don't or else I won't be happy."

Autumn Leaf

A jockey who continually falls off his horse.

"He's an Autumn leaf, never wins a race."

I Feel Stuffed

I'm tired.

"I feel stuffed. I'm going to bed."

No Worries

No problem, forget about it.

"It's ok, no worries mate."

Pommy

An Englishman.

"The new guy at work is a pommy."

Thingo

That thing, what do you call it? A term used for something or someone you can't remeber the name of.

"Pass me over the thingo from the kitchen."

Galah

A noisy foolish person.

"Look at that galah trying to screw it into the wood with a hammer."

Dial

Face.

"Tell your dial to smile."

Maccas

The fast good chain, Mcdonald's.

"Nothing hits the spot like a Maccas."

Dag

A nerd, funny person or goof.

"She's always fooling around, the dag."

Barney

An argument or fight.

"They made up after the barney."

Drum

Information or tip-off.

"I'll give you the drum."

Kark It

To die.

"His grandmother karked it."

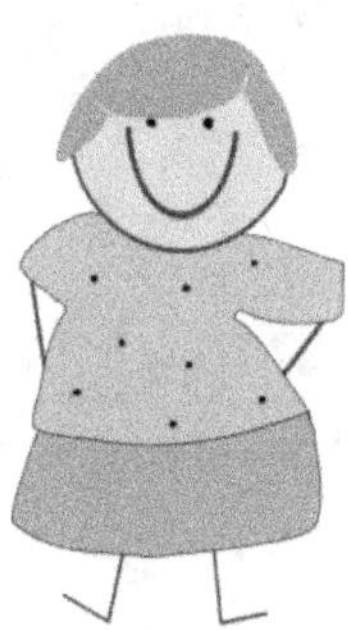

Veg Out

Relax in front of the tv.

"I can't wait to veg out with a cold one."

Battler

Someone working hard and only just making a living.

"She's a battler, working very long hours."

Good Oil

Useful information, a good idea, the truth.

"He's always got the good oil when it comes to the news."

Dingaling

A silly person.

"You're a dingaling."

Mongrel

Despicable person.

"The neighbour is a mongrel mate. He blasts his music first thing in the morning."

Footy

Australian Rules Football.

"We're meeting up to watch the footy tonight."

Plonk

Cheap wine.

"We opened a bottle of plonk and had a good chinwag."

Ocker

An unsophisticated but charming person.

"He's a real ocker despite his moustache."

Push Off

Get lost! get out of here.

"Push off mate."

Cheerio

Goodbye.

"Cheerio for now."

All Froth And No Beer

A wasy to describe someone who is stupid.

"He's all froth and no beer."

Fisho

Fishmonger.

"I'm stopping at the fisho for salmon."

Sleepout

An outdoor area of a house for sleeping.

"The garage is being used as a sleepout."

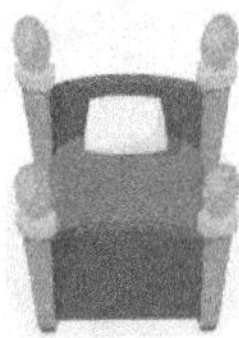

Sweet

Good or we're agreed.

"Sweet - see you at 8pm."

Have A Naughty

Mischievous or naughty behaviour.

"He decided to have a naughty and skip school."

Going Off

Used of a night spot or party that is a lot of fun.

"It was all going off at the party last night."

Standover Man

A large man, usually gang-related, who threatens people with physical violence to have his wishes carried out.

"I bet that standover man is scared of spiders."

Finnegan's Hole

Car trunk.

"Put the esky in Finnegan's hole."

Dork

A person with little personality.

"He's just a dork."

Beaut

Great, fantastic.

"That's beaut."

Pav

Pavlova.

"We're having some pav for dessert."

Noggin

Your head.

"Use your noggin before you act."

Bangers

Sausages.

"Put the bangers on the bbq."

Butcher

Small glass of beer in South Australia.

"Just a butcher for me."

Belly South

Belgrave South, Victoria.

"I've never been to Belly South."

Up Oneself

Have a high opinion of oneself.

"He's so up himself the way he brags about how much he earns."

Donk

It can mean to hit or punch.

"He got a donk in the face."

Lolly

Money.

"I need some lolly!"

Mate

Buddy, friend.

"G'day mate."

<u>Bun In The Oven</u>

Pregnant.

"She's got a bun in the oven."

Bottle Shop

A liquor shop.

"The bottle shop is open."

Beauty

Great, fantastic.

"You beauty!"

Fruitloop

A fool or crazy.

"She missed the bus three times the fruitloop."

Aggro

Aggressive, ticked off, spoiling for a fight.

"What's all this aggo about?"

Buck's Night

A stag party. A male gathering the night before the wedding.

"It's his buck party next week."

Puffed

Out of breath.

"I'm puffed after that jog."

Doodah

A thing with a name that is forgotten.

"What's it called again, the doodah...it's in th bedroom."

Blue

A fight.

"I got into a blue again."

Zonked

To be extremely tired.

"She was zonked after the rellies stayed for the weekend."

Cake Hole

Mouth.

"Shut your cake hole."

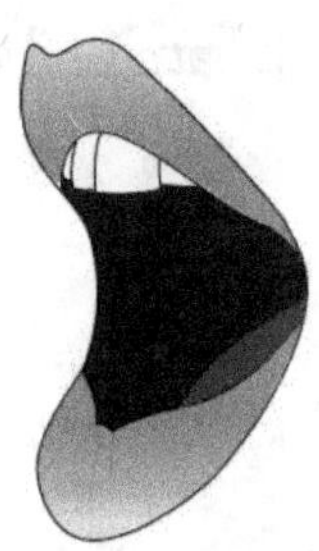

Station

A big farm or grazing property.

"We can go to the station to relax this weekend."

Holy Dooley!

An exclamation of surprise.

"Holey Dooley! I didn't expect to see that."

Garbo

Garbage collector.

"The garbo comes on Mondays."

Bee's Dick

Smallest possible (eg chance of winning something).

"You've got a bee's dick chance of winning the lottery."

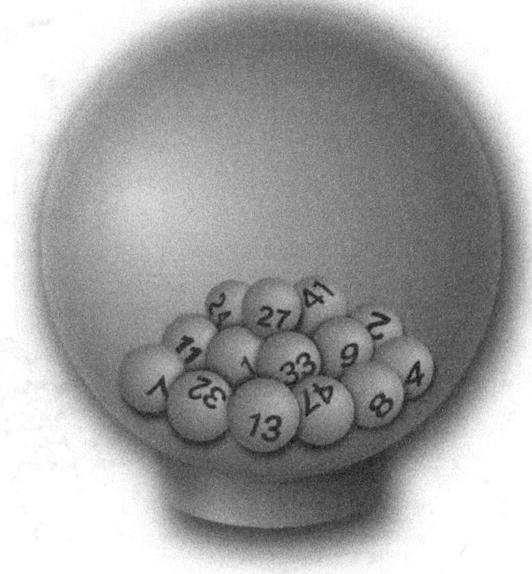

Doco

A documentary.

"Did you see that new doco the other day?"

Dangarang

Awesome.

"Thats's dangarang!"

Flat Out Like A Lizard Drinking

Busy.

"I was flat out like a lizard drinking this arvo."

Freo

Fremantle in Western Australia.

"We're headed to Freo for a cold one."

Fang Carpenter

Dentist.

"I have an appointment with the fang carpenter."

Coat Hanger

Sydney Harbour Bridge.

"It's not too far from the Coat Hanger."

Bloody Oath!

That's certainly true.

"Bloody oath, that's scary."

Big-Note

To brag or boast.

"She was big-noting about her town."

Bushman's Clock

A kookaburra.

"That looks like a bushman's clock."

Chuck A Sickie

Take the day off sick from work when you're feeling perfectly fine and healthy to go in.

"Chuck a sickie if you don't want to go into work today."

Stonkered

Drunk.

"He was so stonkered that he fell asleep at the bar."

Hottie

Hot water bottle.

"I've never used the hottie that I bought."

Sanger

A sandwich.

"I needed a sanga for my brekkie this morning."

<u>**Exercise Book**</u>

School workbook.

"I wrote the story in my exercise book."

<u>**Nipper**</u>

Young surf lifesaver.

"The nippers deserved a day off after a long week."

<u>**Boogie Board**</u>

A hybrid, half-sized surf board.

"He bought a new boogie board."

Copper

Policeman.

"He got a job as a copper."

Aussie Battler

An ordinary Australian trying to make ends meet.

"We're both Aussie battlers with inflation going up."

Pommy Shower

Using deodorant instead of taking a shower.

"You tell he's had a pommy shower by the smell of his BO."

Thongs

Cheap rubber backless sandals.

"If I didn't find my things at the beach, the soles of my feet would have burnt walking back."

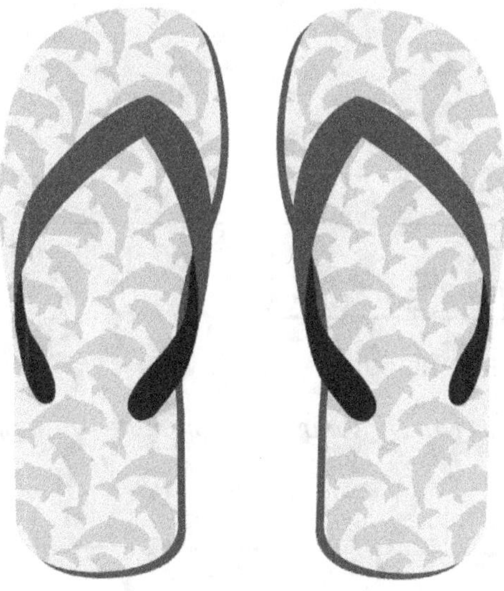

Lollies

Sweets, candy.

"When we stop at the servo, grab a load of lollies."

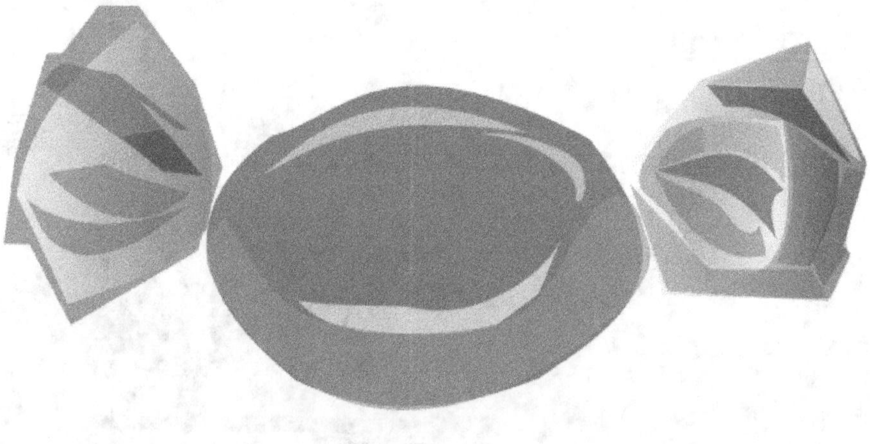

Dill

An idiot.

"The dill tripped over his own feet."

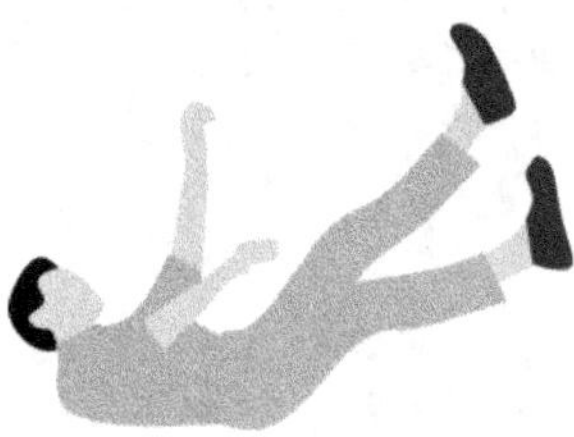

She'll Be Apples

It'll be all right.

"Don't worry about the exam. She'll be apples mate."

Tits On A Bull

To be useless.

"You're as useful as tits on a bull when it comes to advice on ladies."

Porky

Lie.

"Is that another porky?"

Esky

Large insulated food or drink container for picnics, barbecues etc.

"Don't forget to bring the esky."

Dunny Budgie

Blowfly.

"This dunny budgie won't go away."

Pom

An Englishman.

"Our mate is a pom."

Click

One kilometre.

"The park is 2 clicks away."

Milko

Milkman.

"The milko didn't turn up this morning."

Manchester

Household linen.

"I'm in desperate need of some new manchester."

Crikey Mikey

A Snake.

"That's a crikey mikey over there."

Bog In

To commence eating with enthusiasm.

"Bog in to your food."

Chewie

Chewing gum.

"Do you have a chewie?"

Yonks

A long time.

"I haven't seen him in yonks."

Journo

Journalist.

"I wanted to be a journo but decided to become a jackaroo."

Dunny

Outside lavatory.

"Just visiting the dunny."

Bush

The outback or anywhere that isn't in town.

"We're heading out into the bush."

Togs

Swim suit.

"Slip into your togs and enjoy the arvo at the beach."

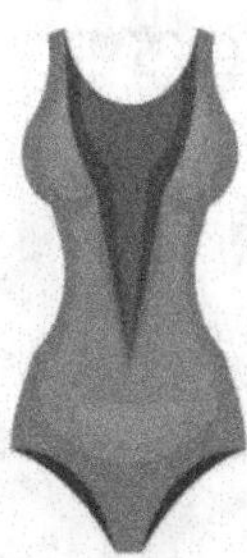

Chalkie

A teacher.

"The chalkie gave her a telling off."

Fair Suck Of The Sav

Exclamation of wonder, awe or disbelief.

"Wow! That's fair suck of the sav mate."

Jumbuck

Sheep.

"Look at those jumbucks in the field."

Bounce

A bully.

"He's always been a bounce."

Yakka

Work.

"I was exhausted after a day of yakka."

Come Off The Grass

Do you think I'm stupid?

"Come off the grass! I'm not falling for that."

Bondi Cigar

A turd in the sea (also brown-eyed mullet).

"I was swimming and nearly got a Bondi cigar in my mouth."

As Full As A Goog

Drunk.

"She was as full as a goog last night."

Alf

A stupid person.

"You're such an Alf mate."

Panel Beater

Car repair shop or person.

"I took my car down to the panel beater to fix the dent."

I'll Be Stuffed

Expression of surprise.

"Well I'll be stuffed."

Cockie

Farmer.

"The cockie let us walk through his land."

Palmy

Palm Beach, New South Wales.

"Palmy is way better than Florida."

Slab

A carton of 24 bottles or cans of beer.

"Remember to pick up a slab of beer for tonight."

Hoof It

To walk rather than take transport.

"Hood it to the bottle shop."

<u>Arvo</u>

Afternoon.

"We're going to the beach this arvo."

<u>Gabba</u>

Wooloongabba - the Brisbane cricket ground.

"I have tickets to watch the cricket match at the Gabba."

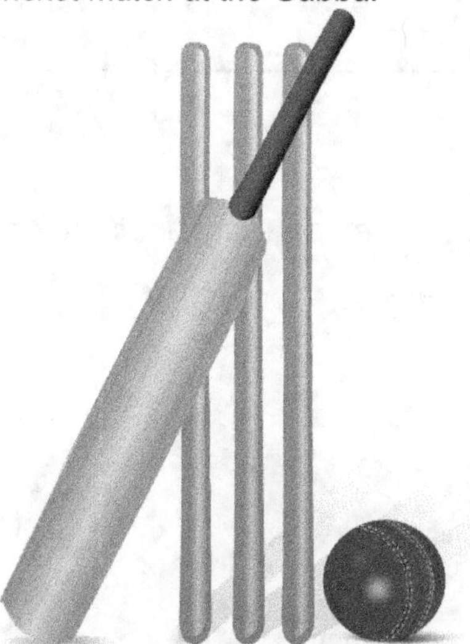

Barbie

Barbecue.

"Fire up the barbie and let's have some bangers."

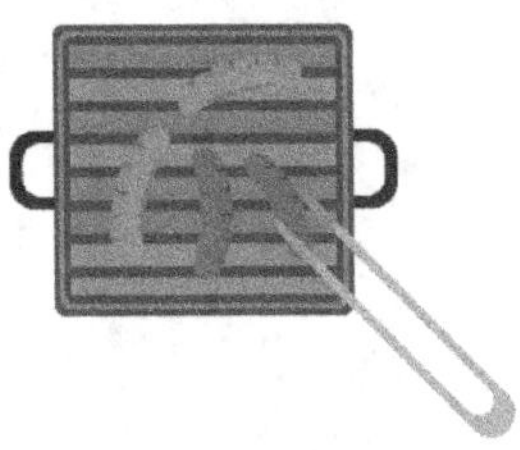

Fossick

Search, rummage.

"I went fossicking through the drawers to find some batteries."

Dudder

An unscrupulous person that cheats others. A conman.

"He looks like a dudder."

Exy

Expensive.

"That's a bit exy for what it is."

Snag

A sausage.

"We had snags and a few cold ones."

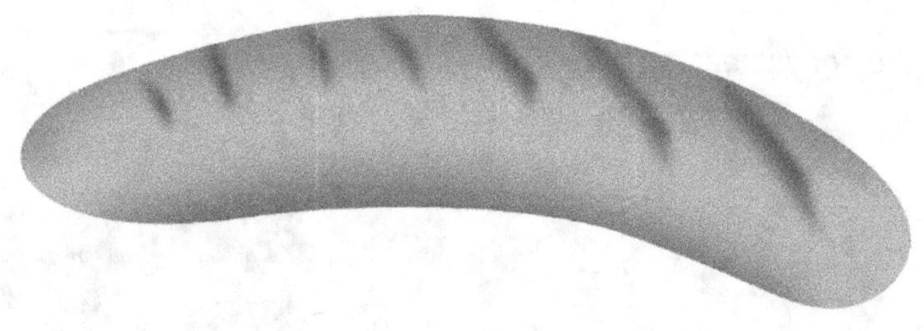

Easy As Pushing Shit Uphill With A Toothpick

Extremely difficult.

"Waking up at in the morning is as easy as pushing shit uphill with a toothpick."

<u>**Grinning Like A Shot Fox**</u>

Very happy, smugly satisfied.

"She was grinning like a shot fox when she returned from her date."

<u>**Vedgies**</u>

Vegetables.

"We need to eat more vedgies with out snags."

<u>**Billy**</u>

A teapot or other container for boiling water.

"Make sure you take a billy for a coffee."

Bull Dust

A lie.

"Don't give me bull dust."

Wowser

A prude person, spoilsport.

"He never smiles, what a wowser."

Milk Bar

A corner shop.

"Go to the milk bar, I need snacks."

Shark Biscuit

Somebody new to surfing.

"You can tell he's a shark biscuit. He fell off the board at least 5 times."

Bush Telly

Campfire.

"I can't wait to watch the bush telly."

Alligator

Horse.

"Get on the alligator."

Liquid Laugh

Vomit.

"I was spewing liquid laugh everywhere this morning."

Croc

A crocodile.

"You don't get crocs in Cranny."

Flat White

Coffee with milk.

"I have a flat white in the morning."

O.S.

Overseas.

"She's O.S. in the States at the moment."

Choppers

Teeth.

"Get your choppers into this pie."

Rag

Local newspaper.

"Seen the front page of the rag today?"

Turps

Alcoholic drink.

"I couldn't stop dancing after I had a couple of turps."

Top End

Far North of Australia.

"He lives near Darwin at the Top End. He's a Top Ender."

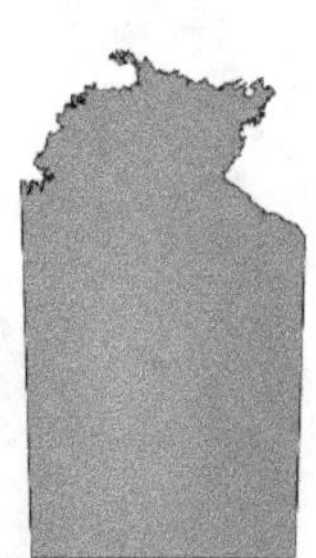

Any Tic Of The Clock

Very soon.

"It'll be here in any tick of the clock."

Budgie smugglers

Men's Speedo-style swimwear.

"Get your budgie smugglers on."

Aussie

Australian.

"This is all about Aussie slang."

Sunnies

Sunglasses.

"I left my sunnies at the beach."

Dog's Eye

Meat pie.

"We're having dog's eye tonight."

Chubbers

Shoes.

"get your chubbers on."

Coldie

A beer.

"I need a coldie."

Chrissie

Christmas.

"It's nearly time for Chrissie."

Ankle biter

A small child.

"Where is the ankle biter?"

<u>**Shit House**</u>

Of poor quality, unenjoyable.

"The concert was shit house mate."

<u>**Vee Dub**</u>

Volkswagen.

"The vee dub is the most reliable car she has owned."

Dux

Top of the class.

"She duxed most of her subjects."

Grundies

Undies, underwear.

"I'm nearly out of clean grundies."

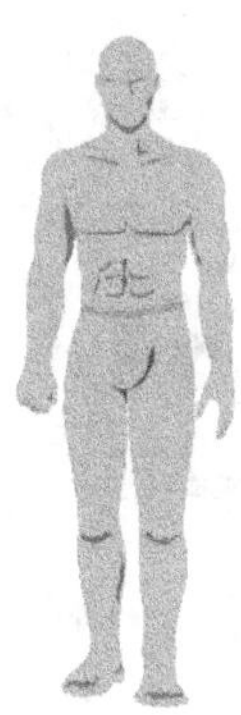

Tucker

Food.

"We grabbed some tucker at the pub."

Smoko

Smoke or coffee break.

"I need to get in a few coffees in my smoko to wake myself up."

Tinny

Can of beer.

"The best think about being down under is opening a tinny in the arvo sun."

Chunder

Vomit.

"I had to pretend to chunder on the phone when I was chucking a sickie."

Relo

Family relative.

"She's visiting a relo in Sydney."

Mappa Tassie

The female pubic region. Similarity in shape with the roughly triangular form of Tasmania.

"Her mappa tassie was the topic of the night at the barbie."

Cactus

Dead, no longer functioning.

"The car is cactus."

<u>Straya</u>

Australia.

"We hope you're learning lots about Straya."

<u>Rack Off</u>

Get lost! get out of here.

"Rack off mate, I'm trying to have a bath here."

<u>Not My Bowl Of Rice</u>

Not my cup of tea or i don't like it.

"She's not my bowl of rice mate."

Cabbie

Taxi driver.

"Ask the cabbie the directions."

Spit The Dummy

Get very upset at something.

"He spat the dummy when he lost the game."

Greenie

An environmentalist.

"She's a greenie, always recycling plastic."

Come The Raw Prawn

To lie or to be generally disagreeable.

"Don't come the raw prawn."

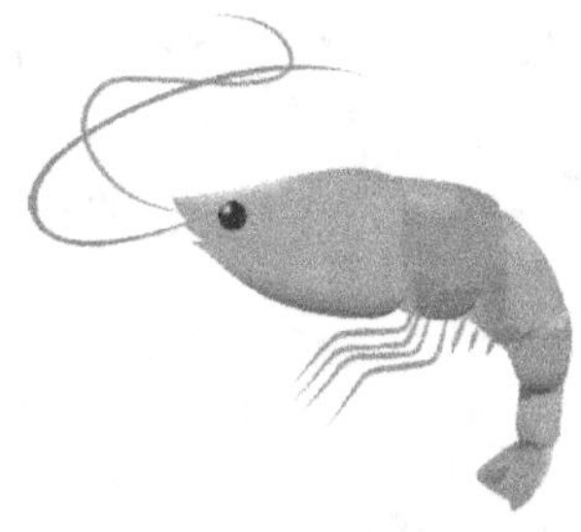

Divvy Van

Police vehicle used for transporting criminals.

"He got taken away in a divvy van."

Grog

liquor, beer.

"We're nearly out of grog."

Roadie

A beverage or snack for consumption when at a gathering or vehicle.

"We all had a roadie for the long drive to Brisbane."

Pozzy

Position.

"I had an amazing view from the pozzy I was in at the match."

Acca Dacca

AC/DC.

"I'm listening to some Acca Dacca."

Skull

To drink a beer in a single draught without taking a breath.

"He is the winner when it comes to skulling beer."

In The Nuddy

Naked.

"It's so hot I feel like being in the nuddy."

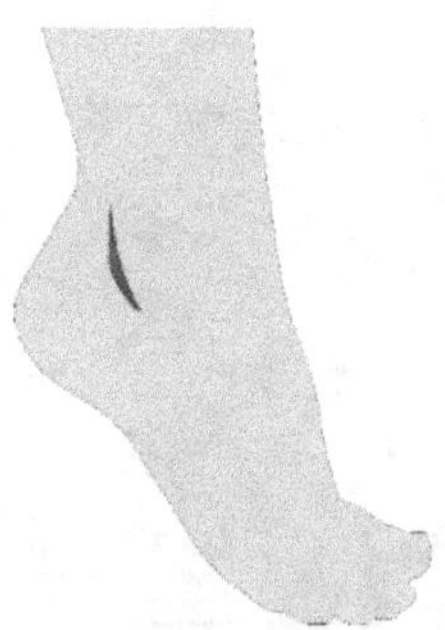

En Zed

New Zealand.

"I would love to go to En Zed."

Yeah Nah

No.

"Do I wanto wake up early? Yeah, nah."

Postie

Postman, mailman.

"The postie hasn't been yet."

Squid Ink

When someone burns sausages or other food on a barbie.

"There's more than a little squid ink on this snag."

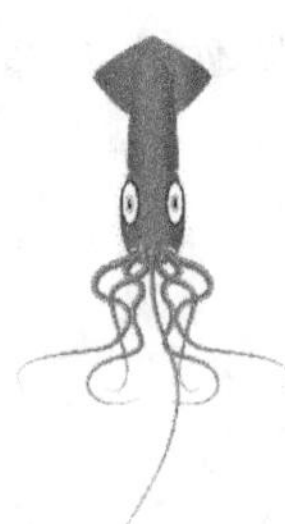

Walkabout

A hike or long walk.

"He went walkabout after he lost his job."

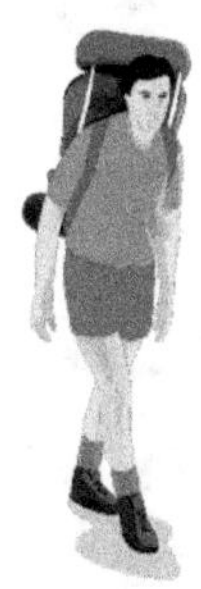

Idiot Box

Television.

"I've been in front of the idiot box all day."

Icy Pole

Popsicle, lollypop.

"Get an ice pole from the freezer to cool me down."

Pig's Arse

I don't agree with you.

"Pig's arse it's gonna rain tomorrow."

Tall Poppy Syndrome

The tendency to criticise successful people.

"You'll be the victim of tall poppy syndrome if you advertise your success."

Spunk

A good looking person of either sex.

"He's a real spunk. Wow!"

Bean Counter

An accountant.

"Congratulations on qualifying as a bean counter."

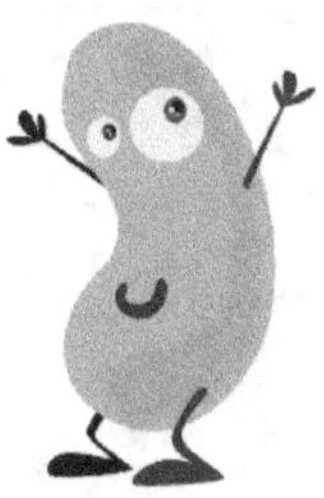

Cleanskin

Cattle that have not been branded, earmarked or castrated.

"That's one of my cleanskins."

Stubby

A cold beer bottle.

"I'm ready for a stubby and a night of relaxation."

Crook

Sick or badly made.

"The sauce pan was crook."

Kiwi

A person from New Zealand.

"Foreigners can't tell the difference between an Aussie and a Kiwi."

Billy Lids

The kids.

"The billy lids were too loud this morning."

Dip

Swim.

"Let's take a dip in the pool."

Date Roll

Roll of toilet paper.

"We're out of date roll."

Woop Woop

Middle of nowhere.

"We broke down out in woop woop."

Yewy

A U-turn.

"Do a yewy over there."

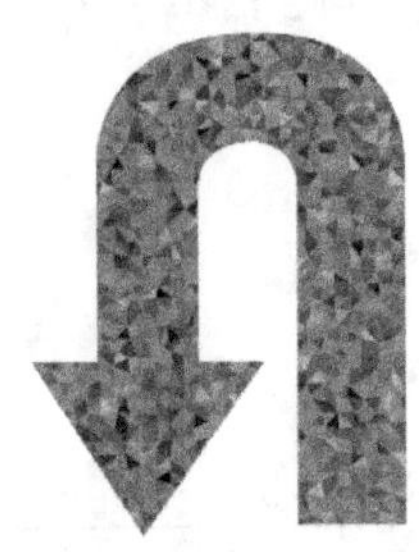

Rage On

To continue partying.

"We decided to rage on well into Saturday morning."

Elephant's Trunk

Rhyming slang for drunk.

"She was elephant's trunk again."

Stoked

Very pleased.

"I'm stoked to be visiting Oz."

Deadset

True.

"Deadset you've got a nice tan."

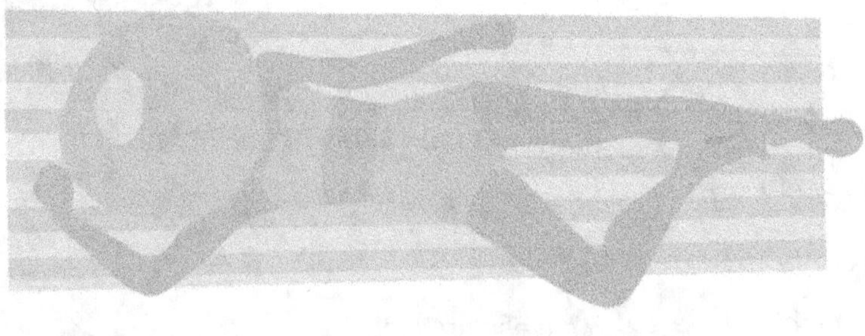

Lead Foot

Someone who drives fast.

"That woman has a lead foot, always in a hurry when she's driving."

Fair Dinkum

True, real, genuine.

"That's a fair dinkum chook."

Cane Toad

A person from Queensland.

"The Cane Toad said it wasn't raining."

White Pointers

Topless female sunbathers.

"You get plenty of white pointers on this side of the beach."

Banana Bender

A person from Queensland.

"He sounds like a banana bender."

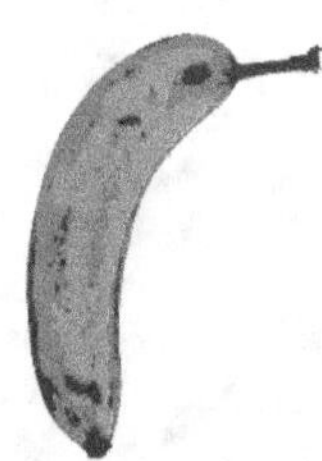

Bottle-O

A liquor shop.

"I'm going to the Bottle-O on the way back."

Servo

Petrol station.

"Pick up some snacks from the servo on your home."

Dogereedoo

A puppy.

"The dogereedoo is so cute."

Cozzie

A swimming costume.

"That cozzie looks nice on you."

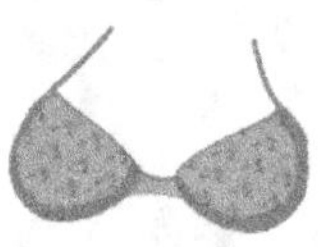

Bats

Crazy.

"She was going bats."

Pash

A long passionate kiss.

"Did you see them pash at the party?"

<u>**Bush Oyster**</u>

Nasal mucus.

"Clean yourself up, you have bush oyster everywhere."

<u>**Centralia**</u>

The inland region of Australia.

"I've never been to Centralia."

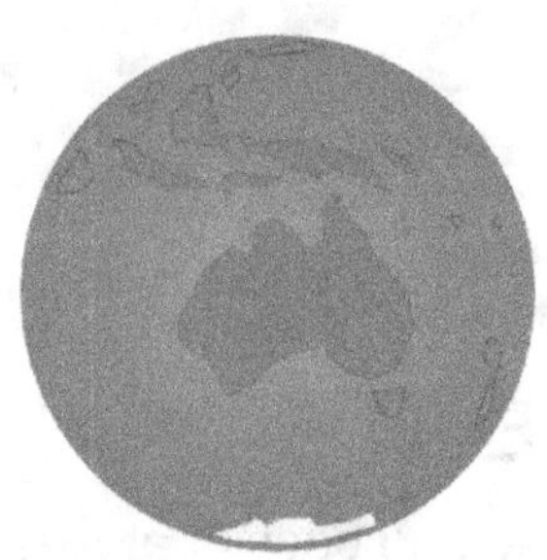

<u>**Bonza**</u>

A term to describe something as excellent.

"Your results are really bonza!"

Cockie

Cockatoo.

"That sounds like a cockie."

Buck

One dollar - $1.

"I'm a Buck short."

Ivories

Your teeth.

"I'm going to brush the ovories then head to bed."

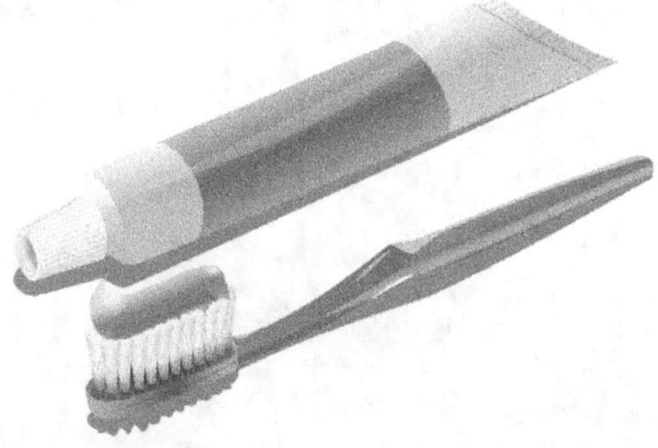

Water The Horse

To urinate.

"Stay here whilst I water the horse."

Bag Of Fruit

Rhyming slang for suit.

"Put on your bag of fruit and be there at 6pm."

Pack A Wallop

Punch someone hard.

"I'll pack a wallop if you don't behave yourself."

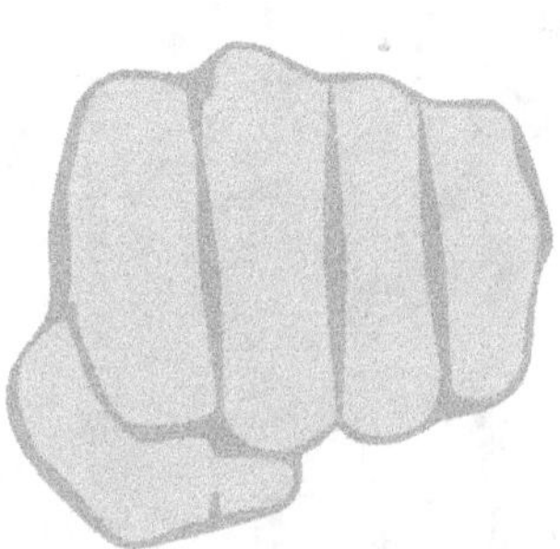

Bikkie

A biscuit.

"Pass the bikkies over."

Down The John

Off to the toilet.

"I need to go down the John."

Farmer Giles

Rhyming slang for piles or haemorroids.

"I can't sit down because of the Farmer Giles."

Cockroach

A person from New South Wales.

"The cockroach came here for a few days."

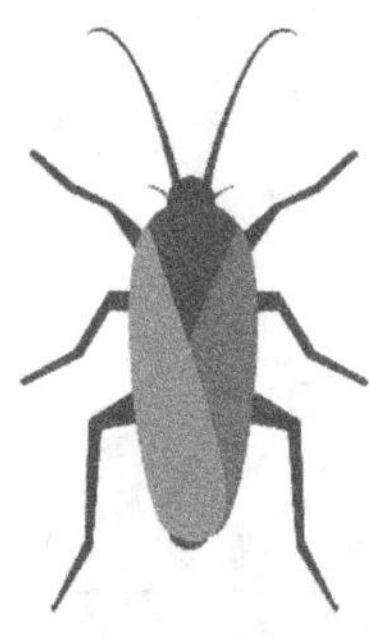

Egg Beater

A helicopter.

"The egg beater was flying over the house again."

Amber Fluid

Beer.

"We need to get some amber fluid down us."

Bunch Of Fives

A punch or fist.

"If you'r not careful you'll get a bunch of fives."

Ginger Meggs

Rhyming slang for legs.

"I can see you gave your ginger meggs a shave."

Rapt

Pleased, delighted.

"I got the job. I'm so rapt right now."

Good Onya

Good for you, well done.

"Good onya for fixing it and making it work."

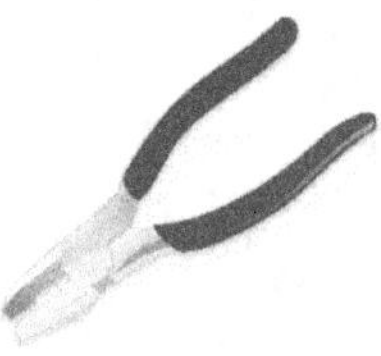

Apple Eater

Someone from Tasmania.

"He's an apple eater."

G'day

Hello.

"G'day mate, what a beautiful day."

<u>**Ute**</u>

Utility vehicle, pickup truck.

"Let's go out to the bush in the ute."

<u>**Sunbake**</u>

Sunbathe.

"Have a sunbake whilst I get you a stubby."

<u>**Earbashing**</u>

Nagging, non-stop chatter.

"I got a right earbashing when I met up with her."

His Blood's Worth Bottling

He's an excellent, helpful bloke.

"He's such a nice guy. His blood's worth bottling."

"He's such a nice guy. His blood's worth bottling."